10 EXPLORERS WHO CHANGED THE WORLD

Written by Clive Gifford
Illustrated by David Cousens

KINGFISHER
NEW YORK

Copyright © 2008 by Macmillan Children's Books
KINGFISHER
Published in the United States by Kingfisher, an imprint of Henry Holt
and Company LLC, 175 Fifth Avenue, New York, New York 10010. First
published in Great Britain by Kingfisher Publications plc, an imprint of
Macmillan Children's Books, London.

Distributed in Canada by H. B. Fenn and Company Ltd.

Library of Congress Cataloging-in-Publication Data
Gifford, Clive.
  Ten explorers who changed the world / Clive Gifford.—1st
American ed.
      p. cm.
  Includes index.
  ISBN 978-0-7534-6103-7
  1. Discoveries in geography—Juvenile literature. 2. Explorers—Juvenile
literature. I. Title.
  G175.G49 2008
  910.92'2--dc22

                                2007047477

ISBN: 978-0-7534-6103-7

Kingfisher books are available for special promotions and premiums.
For details contact: Director of Special Markets, Holtzbrinck Publishers.

First American Edition October 2008
Printed in Singapore
10 9 8 7 6 5 4 3 2 1
1TR/0308/TWP/MAR/150MA/C

James Cook

Alexander
von Humboldt

Christopher
Columbus

Contents

The first explorers

People have always been curious about what lies just out of view beyond the horizon. In the distant past, many peoples—Native Americans, Aborigines, and Bedouin Arabs, for example—were nomadic, wandering long distances in search of good hunting lands.

The first known organized exploration began almost 5,000 years ago, when the ancient Egyptians voyaged down the Red Sea to reach the mysterious land of Punt, which was probably in eastern Africa.

As they developed ships, seafaring peoples, such as the Phoenicians of the Middle East, became traders. They explored the Mediterranean Sea and parts of the Atlantic Ocean. In around 480 B.C. the famous Phoenician explorer Hanno sailed along the west coast of Africa almost as far south as the equator.

The Polynesians, who lived in the Pacific Ocean islands, were intrepid explorers. From around 2,200 years ago, groups of Polynesians left Samoa and Tonga in large canoes. Without compasses or maps, they gradually crossed the huge Pacific Ocean to settle in Tahiti by A.D. 300, Hawaii by A.D. 500, and New Zealand by A.D. 850.

Many early explorers were military leaders who wanted to conquer other peoples and lands. In the 4th century B.C., Alexander the Great of Macedonia explored Egypt, the Middle East, and northern India. Roman leader Julius Caesar conquered lands in northern and Western Europe in the 1st century A.D. Seven hundred years later, the Vikings of Scandinavia began to launch raids into the Mediterranean, Baltic, and Caspian seas. The most famous Viking voyagers headed west across the Atlantic Ocean. They reached Iceland by A.D. 860, Greenland 120 years later, and North America in around A.D. 1002.

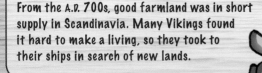

From the A.D. 700s, good farmland was in short supply in Scandinavia. Many Vikings found it hard to make a living, so they took to their ships in search of new lands.

To the east, Ibn Battuta was a legendary Muslim adventurer. After making a religious pilgrimage from Morocco to Mecca (Saudi Arabia), he continued moving. Between 1325 and 1354, he traveled more than 74,000 mi. (120,000km) through Africa, Russia, China, and Sri Lanka. His famous book about these adventures, *The Travels of Ibn Battuta*, can still be read today.

Ibn Battuta traveled by sea and over land, often trekking across deserts as part of a caravan of camels.

LIFE LINK
Turn the page to read the amazing story of Marco Polo, the first in the list of ten explorers who changed the world. At the end of his story, look for a "Life Link" box like this one—it will explain what connects Marco Polo to the next explorer in the chain.

Marco Polo

Winter 1298. Author Rustichello da Pisa had languished in jail for 14 years following his capture by Genoese forces at the Battle of Meloria. Sitting in his cell, he listened with wonder to the tales of a new inmate, Marco Polo, who had been been arrested by the Genoese while sailing on a Venetian galley ship.

Three years had passed since Polo's return from a series of epic journeys in Asia. After his release from prison in 1299, he settled down to a quiet, prosperous life as a merchant in Venice, Italy. With the help of Rustichello, his story was eventually published as *The Travels of Marco Polo*. The tales would excite travelers and explorers for years to come.

Exploration was in Polo's blood. He was born in Venice, one of medieval Europe's wealthiest cities. When he was six years old, his father, Niccolo, and uncle Maffeo set off for Asia. Marco was 15 years old by the time they returned. Two years later, he joined his father and uncle on their second journey to Asia. Marco would not see Venice again for 24 years.

Rustichello da Pisa, a writer from Umbria in northern Italy, listens to Marco Polo. Their book about the explorer's travels was a big success in medieval Europe.

The Silk Road was a collection of trade routes that stretched from the Black Sea to deep inside China. The Polos traveled along parts of the Silk Road on their journey east.

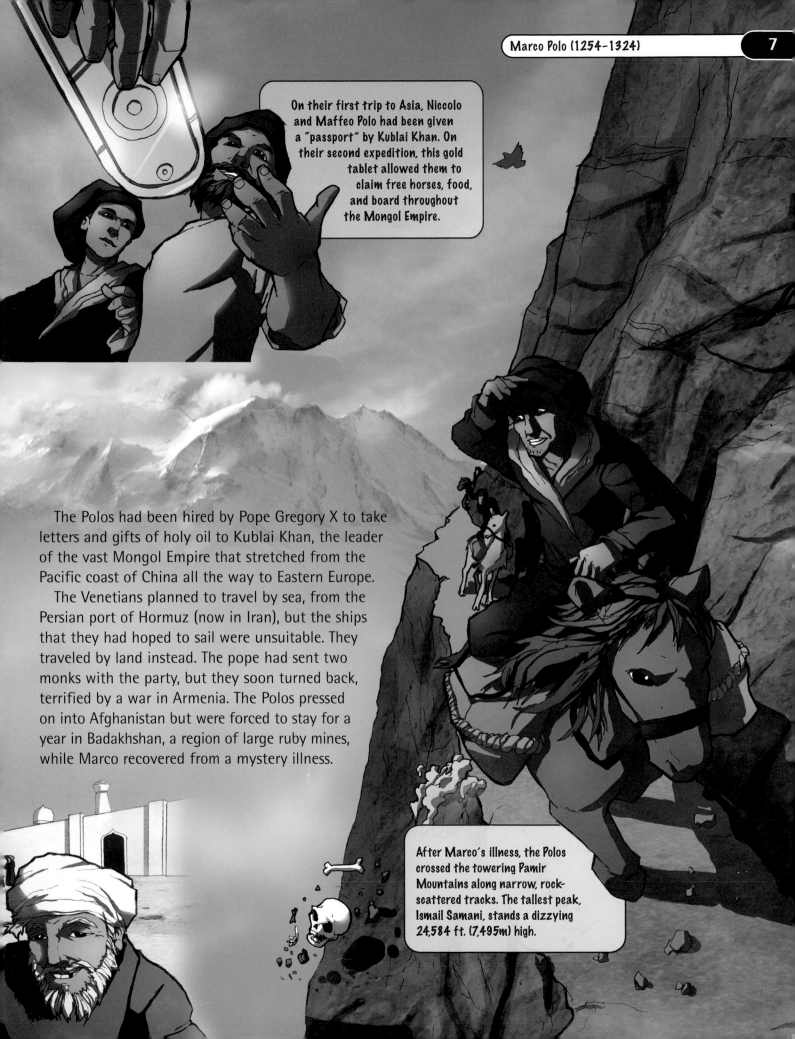

On their first trip to Asia, Niccolo and Maffeo Polo had been given a "passport" by Kublai Khan. On their second expedition, this gold tablet allowed them to claim free horses, food, and board throughout the Mongol Empire.

The Polos had been hired by Pope Gregory X to take letters and gifts of holy oil to Kublai Khan, the leader of the vast Mongol Empire that stretched from the Pacific coast of China all the way to Eastern Europe.

The Venetians planned to travel by sea, from the Persian port of Hormuz (now in Iran), but the ships that they had hoped to sail were unsuitable. They traveled by land instead. The pope had sent two monks with the party, but they soon turned back, terrified by a war in Armenia. The Polos pressed on into Afghanistan but were forced to stay for a year in Badakhshan, a region of large ruby mines, while Marco recovered from a mystery illness.

After Marco's illness, the Polos crossed the towering Pamir Mountains along narrow, rock-scattered tracks. The tallest peak, Ismail Samani, stands a dizzying 24,584 ft. (7,495m) high.

It took the Polos one month to cross the Gobi Desert. Marco was struck by its vast size and lack of life.

The Polos are thought to have skirted the Taklimakan Desert to Lop Nur and then crossed the hostile Gobi Desert. In Karakhoja, on the other side, Marco saw a cloth that survived being thrown onto a fire. He was so impressed with this material, which he called *salamander* (today we know it as asbestos), that a sample was taken as a gift for Pope Gregory X.

The Mongols were highly organized and knew about the travelers' impending arrival far in advance. Around 40 days' trek from Kublai Khan's summer palace, the Polos were greeted by escorts who led them to the emperor in the city of Shangdu, almost 200 mi. (300km) northwest of the present-day capital of China, Beijing. It was 1275, and the Polos had traveled 5,000 mi. (8,000km) in three and a half years.

The Mongols had been a loose group of nomadic tribes before Gengis Khan, the founder of the Mongol Empire, brought them together. Their terrifying and fearless warriors were armed with bows, lances, and curved swords called scimitars.

During the journey, Marco had turned from a teenager into a man. He had a gift for foreign languages and soon became popular with the Mongol leader. The Polos were employed in the service of Kublai Khan, Marco as a diplomat and tax inspector. He traveled throughout the empire, visiting many parts of China, Mongolia, Tibet, and Burma (Myanmar). He was amazed by what he saw—"handsome lions streaked with white, black, and red stripes" (tigers), the city of Hangzhou with its "12,000 bridges," and paper currency at a time when Europeans used only coins. "With these pieces of paper they can buy anything," he marveled.

Marco was in awe of Khanbalik, the capital city of the Mongol Empire. According to his book, each of its gates was guarded by 1,000 men, and more than 1,000 carts of expensive silk would pass through them every day. The grand hall of the immense marble palace could seat 6,000 guests for a feast.

Seventeen years passed and Kublai Khan reached his 70th birthday. The Polos pleaded to be allowed to return to Venice, partly owing to fear that the emperor's eventual successor would turn against them. Reluctantly, Kublai Khan agreed and provided a fleet of 14 grand ships.

Marco Polo was astonished to see that elephants were used in large numbers by hunters and also by the soldiers of Kublai Khan's armies.

Marco bows at the feet of Kublai Khan, the grandson of Gengis and the fifth ruler of the Mongol Empire.

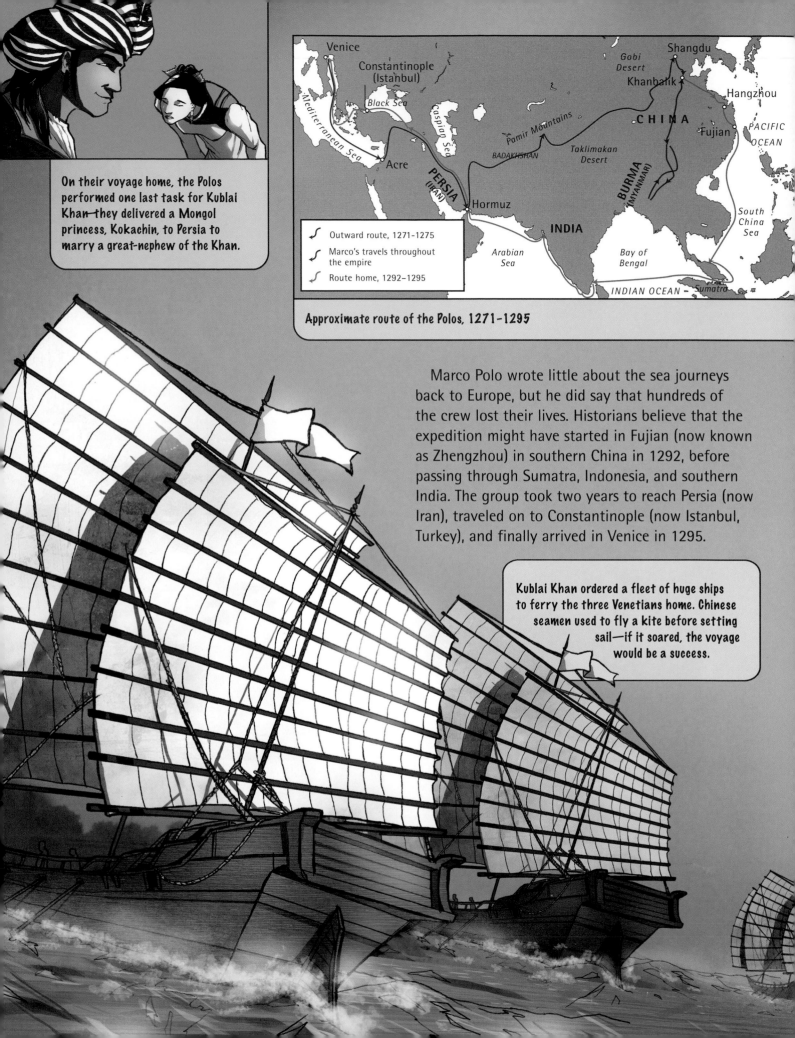

On their voyage home, the Polos performed one last task for Kublai Khan—they delivered a Mongol princess, Kokachin, to Persia to marry a great-nephew of the Khan.

Approximate route of the Polos, 1271–1295

Venice
Constantinople (Istanbul)
Black Sea
Mediterranean Sea
Acre
Caspian Sea
PERSIA (IRAN)
Hormuz
Arabian Sea
INDIA
Bay of Bengal
Pamir Mountains
BADAKHSHAN
Taklimakan Desert
Gobi Desert
Shangdu
Khanbalik
CHINA
Hangzhou
Fujian
PACIFIC OCEAN
BURMA (MYANMAR)
South China Sea
INDIAN OCEAN — Sumatra

〰 Outward route, 1271–1275
〰 Marco's travels throughout the empire
〰 Route home, 1292–1295

Marco Polo wrote little about the sea journeys back to Europe, but he did say that hundreds of the crew lost their lives. Historians believe that the expedition might have started in Fujian (now known as Zhengzhou) in southern China in 1292, before passing through Sumatra, Indonesia, and southern India. The group took two years to reach Persia (now Iran), traveled on to Constantinople (now Istanbul, Turkey), and finally arrived in Venice in 1295.

Kublai Khan ordered a fleet of huge ships to ferry the three Venetians home. Chinese seamen used to fly a kite before setting sail—if it soared, the voyage would be a success.

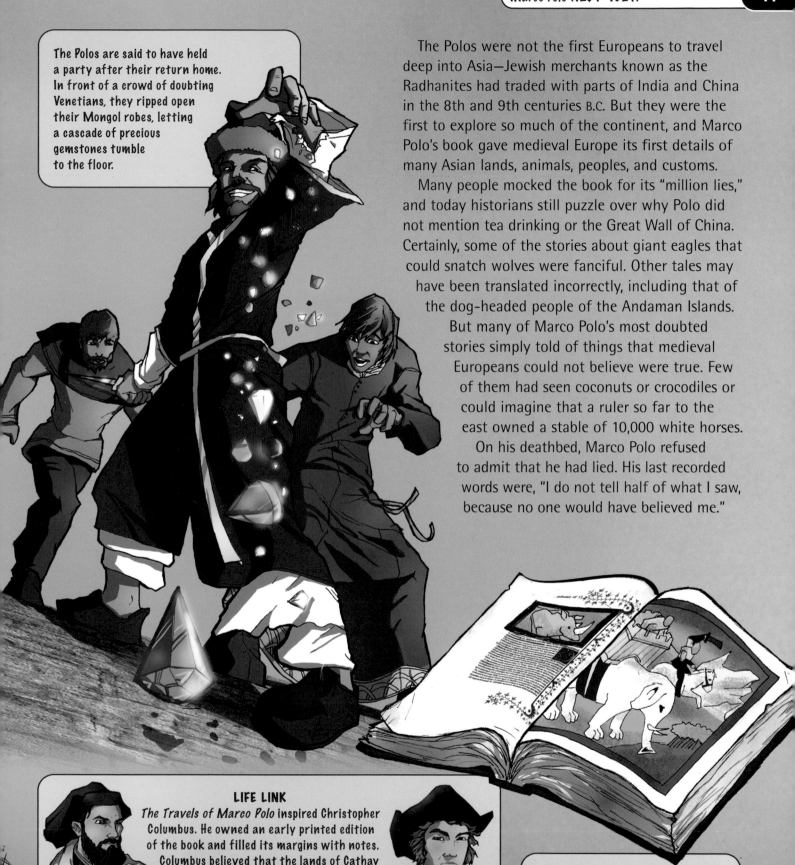

The Polos are said to have held a party after their return home. In front of a crowd of doubting Venetians, they ripped open their Mongol robes, letting a cascade of precious gemstones tumble to the floor.

The Polos were not the first Europeans to travel deep into Asia—Jewish merchants known as the Radhanites had traded with parts of India and China in the 8th and 9th centuries B.C. But they were the first to explore so much of the continent, and Marco Polo's book gave medieval Europe its first details of many Asian lands, animals, peoples, and customs.

Many people mocked the book for its "million lies," and today historians still puzzle over why Polo did not mention tea drinking or the Great Wall of China. Certainly, some of the stories about giant eagles that could snatch wolves were fanciful. Other tales may have been translated incorrectly, including that of the dog-headed people of the Andaman Islands. But many of Marco Polo's most doubted stories simply told of things that medieval Europeans could not believe were true. Few of them had seen coconuts or crocodiles or could imagine that a ruler so far to the east owned a stable of 10,000 white horses. On his deathbed, Marco Polo refused to admit that he had lied. His last recorded words were, "I do not tell half of what I saw, because no one would have believed me."

LIFE LINK
The Travels of Marco Polo inspired Christopher Columbus. He owned an early printed edition of the book and filled its margins with notes. Columbus believed that the lands of Cathay (China) and Cipango (Japan) that Polo described could be reached by sailing west rather than traveling overland to the east.

Early editions of Polo's book were copied by hand. The first printed edition was published in 1477.

Christopher Columbus

August 1476. Christopher Columbus, a 25-year-old man from the Italian city-state of Genoa, clung to an oar and prayed. He had just had his first taste of sailing in the Atlantic Ocean. Now he was trying to survive in its cold waters. Serving on a Genoese merchant fleet, his ship had been attacked and set on fire 6 mi. (10km) off the coast of Portugal. Slowly, Columbus struggled ashore.

Columbus's ship, part of a fleet of five vessels, might have been attacked by the notorious French pirate Guillaume Casenove Coulon.

Columbus headed to the Portuguese capital, Lisbon, to join his brother, Bartholomew. The pair made a living as mapmakers and merchants. During trading voyages to Ireland and west Africa, Columbus began to develop his own theories of navigation. Gold, spices, and glory seemed to lie wherever new lands were discovered. The overland routes to India and Cathay (China) were long and dangerous, while the African coast seemed never-ending—but what, Columbus wondered, lay to the west of Portugal, beyond the Atlantic Ocean?

When Columbus asked the Spanish court to support his voyage, he insisted that he be awarded the rank of *Admiral of the Ocean Seas*, made governor of any lands he found, and receive one tenth of all profits.

Marco Polo's tales of golden temples and great riches in the lands of Cathay and Cipango (Japan) greatly excited Columbus. He hungrily collected maps, charts, and stories and concocted a plan to reach the "Indies" (the Far East) by sailing west. Columbus calculated that Cipango lay 2,700 mi. (4,400km) beyond the Canary Islands, a distance that some Portuguese ships had already sailed. In reality, that distance is more than four times greater.

Columbus presented his plans to King John II of Portugal in 1484, but he was turned down. Eventually he struck a deal with Spain, Portugal's fierce rival, and on August 12, 1492, a fleet of three ships set sail from Palos. Columbus commanded the *Santa Maria*; the Pinzon brothers, Vicente and Martin, captained the *Nina* and the *Pinta*.

Columbus was happy with the *Nina* and the *Pinta*, which were small and fast. But his flagship, the *Santa Maria*, was a much heavier vessel. Its one advantage was a large hold that was crammed with supplies for the voyage into the unknown.

The 90 or so crew members soon became restless. Many were suspicious of Columbus because he was a Genoan who had lived in Portugal, Spain's enemy. Tension grew as the weeks passed. Again and again there were false alarms that the coast was in sight, partly because a reward of 10,000 *maravedis* per year (equal to around ten months' pay) was on offer to the first man to spot land.

A minor mutiny broke out on the *Santa Maria* on October 10. Columbus stopped it by promising to turn back if land had not been sighted within two days. His log revealed, however, that he had no intention of doing so. To calm his nervous crew, Columbus lied about how far they had traveled that day, just as he had on previous days.

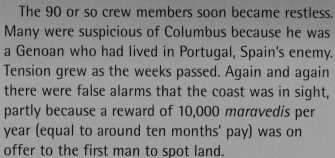

With no crew's quarters below deck, sailors often tied themselves to the ship to avoid being washed overboard as they slept.

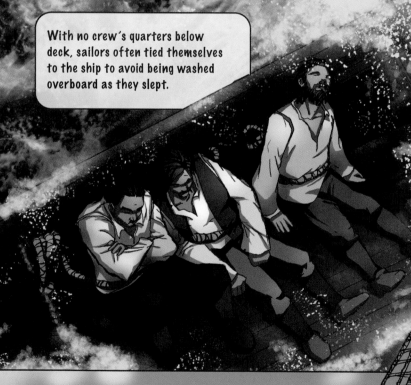

Onboard, fights often broke out between sailors from different families or regions. Some of the crew were criminals who had joined the expedition in return for pardons for their wrongdoings.

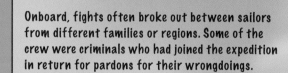

Rodrigo de Triana was the first to spot land, stationed high above the deck in the crow's-nest of the *Pinta*.

As the deadline loomed, a cry rang out: "Land! Land!" It was October 12, 1492. Columbus led the landing party, planting flags, praying, and giving thanks. The voyage had taken only 33 days from the Canary Islands. Columbus was sure that he had reached an island east of Cipango. In fact, he stood on one of the Bahamian islands in the Caribbean, but to this day we are unsure which one.

The expedition landed on an island known by the local peoples as Guanahani. Columbus claimed the island for Spain and renamed it San Salvador.

Columbus set sail three days later, anxious to reach lands with greater riches. He explored the coast of Cuba but did not find the wealth that he had expected. In late November, Martin Pinzon, the captain of the *Pinta*, abandoned the other two ships to search for gold. Columbus sailed for an island that the local peoples called Bohio, hoping that it was Cathay or Cipango. It was actually the large island now occupied by Haiti and the Dominican Republic. Columbus named it La Isla Española; we call it Hispaniola. There, Columbus obtained small pieces of gold and collected pineapples and turkeys, both unknown in Europe. But on Christmas Day 1492, the *Santa Maria* ran aground on a reef. With only one ship remaining, almost 40 crew members were left behind on Hispaniola to build a fort in La Navidad, mostly from the wreck of the *Santa Maria*.

In San Salvador, Columbus gave glass beads and other items to the native peoples in return for javelin spears, balls of cotton, and parrots.

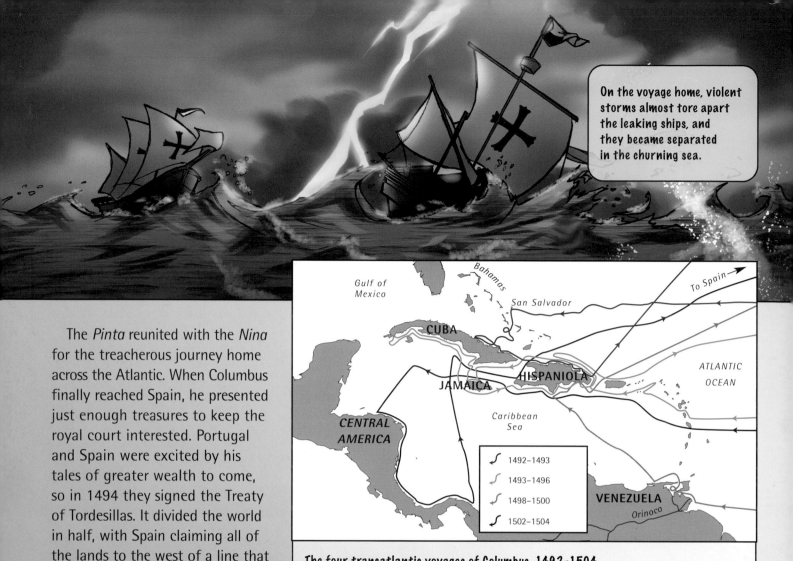

On the voyage home, violent storms almost tore apart the leaking ships, and they became separated in the churning sea.

Gulf of Mexico

Bahamas

San Salvador

CUBA

HISPANIOLA

JAMAICA

CENTRAL AMERICA

Caribbean Sea

To Spain →

ATLANTIC OCEAN

VENEZUELA

Orinoco

1492–1493
1493–1496
1498–1500
1502–1504

The four transatlantic voyages of Columbus, 1492–1504

The *Pinta* reunited with the *Nina* for the treacherous journey home across the Atlantic. When Columbus finally reached Spain, he presented just enough treasures to keep the royal court interested. Portugal and Spain were excited by his tales of greater wealth to come, so in 1494 they signed the Treaty of Tordesillas. It divided the world in half, with Spain claiming all of the lands to the west of a line that ran through the Atlantic.

Columbus made three more Atlantic voyages. During his expedition of 1493–1496, he named many Caribbean islands, including Dominica, Antigua, and Jamaica. From 1498 to 1500, he traveled farther south to the coast of Venezuela, where he was astonished by the giant mouth of the Orinoco River. He did not explore it further, however, and returned to the Spanish colony on Hispaniola to exert his authority on both the colonists and the local peoples, many of whom were shipped to Europe as slaves.

Columbus became a hero after his first voyage. Although he returned without cloves, ginger, or other spices, he did present to the king and queen previously unknown items including pineapples, turkeys, and a hammock.

As the governor of Hispaniola, Columbus ordered thousands of Taino people to be enslaved.

Columbus set sail on his final voyage in 1502. He landed in Central America but ignored local stories of great inland empires. Without knowing it, he was close to the mighty Aztec and Inca civilizations. Later, the explorer's ship fell apart on the island of Jamaica, marooning the crew for one year before their return to Spain in 1504. The strain took its toll on Columbus, and he died two years later.

The following decades saw a scramble for riches in South and Central America. Before Columbus, Spain's only overseas territory had been the Canary Islands. One hundred years later, it boasted an enormous and profitable empire.

Columbus had many flaws—he played a part in starting the Caribbean slave trade and he wrongly believed that he had reached the Far East. Yet it was Columbus alone who took a giant step into the unknown by sailing westward and opening up a whole new world.

Within **35** years of Columbus's death, Spanish soldiers and explorers known as conquistadors had conquered the Aztec and Inca civilizations in search of gold and other riches.

Columbus was arrested in **1500** after the colonists had complained about his harsh rule as the governor. He was taken to Spain in chains but later released.

LIFE LINK
Columbus's proposal to sail to the Indies was turned down by the king of Portugal, John II. John's successor, King Manuel I, rejected Ferdinand Magellan's similar plan. Both explorers took their services to Spain, where they had to win the approval of the powerful Bishop Juan Rodríguez de Fonseca before they could set sail.

Ferdinand Magellan

"Serve whom you will, Clubfoot. It is a matter of indifference to us." The king of Portugal's words rang in Ferdinand Magellan's ears as he limped away. With mocking laughter from the courtiers, the king had delivered the ultimate snub—withdrawing his hands to prevent Magellan from bowing and kissing them, as was the custom of the time. The country that Magellan had served since childhood had turned its back on him. It was October 1516, he was almost 40 years old, and his dreams of exploration seemed to be over . . .

Magellan had walked with a limp ever since his knee was shattered by an Arab lance in the city of Azemmour in Morocco.

Because spices sold for high prices, Magellan wanted to find a sea route to the parts of Asia where they grew.

As a young boy, Magellan had arrived at Portugal's royal court in 1492, the year that Columbus sailed from Spain. He was educated as a pageboy by a duke, Dom Manuel, who took an instant dislike to him. Magellan served at court for many years, until, in 1505, he went to sea with a Portuguese fleet that used brute force to plunder riches in Africa and Asia. He returned home in 1514 to find that Dom Manuel had been crowned King Manuel I. Two years later, the scornful king rejected Magellan's plan for a voyage to the East Indies.

Instead of giving up, Magellan defected to Portugal's deadly rival, Spain. He might have taken with him secret charts that showed that the valuable spices of Southeast Asia could be reached by sailing west through the Americas. He struggled to convince the Spanish, who suspected that he was a madman or a spy and were afraid of angering the Portuguese. But eventually, King Charles I of Spain agreed to fund the voyage.

> As Magellan prepared the five ships, his crew complained about their low pay and were unhappy even before the expedition set off.

Magellan's fleet of five ships sailed from the Spanish city of Seville on August 10, 1519. Onboard were 277 men, many of whom were Spanish and wary of their Portuguese leader. After five weeks anchored in Spanish waters for fear of Portuguese attacks, the fleet set sail for the Canary Islands.

Just as his father had attempted to thwart Columbus, King Manuel I sent ships to intercept Magellan, but without success. As the expedition crossed the Atlantic Ocean, the crew muttered darkly about Magellan, and the Spanish captain, Juan de Cartagena, was arrested for plotting a mutiny.

> Magellan's flagship, *Trinidad*, sails west, flanked by the *San Antonio*, *Concepción*, *Victoria*, and *Santiago*.

> One of Magellan's sailors was an Italian scholar named Antonio Pigafetta. His journals provided a detailed record of the voyage.

The fleet scoured the coast of South America, seeking a route west. They sailed down the Río de la Plata, mistakenly thinking that the river was a passage to the Indies. At this point Magellan knew that his charts were wrong. He sailed south into violent seas and hailstorms that battered the ships, while ice frosted the rigging faster than the sailors could hack it away.

In March 1520, the fleet landed in a desolate bay in southern Argentina. Magellan named it Port Saint Julian. He ordered his crew to build huts and repair the ships. Rations were cut to last throughout the southern winter and morale was low. For months, captains Cartagena, Mendoza, and Quesada had been plotting. Now they acted, stealing three ships and leaving Magellan outnumbered. But they underestimated their leader's cunning . . .

A sailor tries to catch a penguin in Patagonia, southern Argentina. Magellan's men are thought to have been the first Europeans to see these birds.

Magellan crushed the mutiny within two days. He was lenient with some of the mutineers, but the ringleaders did not escape his wrath. He ordered Quesada to be killed by his own secretary, who begged for forgiveness as he beheaded the captain. The bodies of Quesada and Mendoza were chopped into pieces and displayed as a grisly warning to the others; Cartagena was condemned to a slow death, marooned at Port Saint Julian. As the fleet sailed away, no one onboard doubted who was in command.

Rounding Cape Virgenes on November 1, 1520, Magellan finally found what he had been searching for. The Strait of Magellan, which he called All Saints' Channel, forms a route between the icy islands of Tierra del Fuego and the southern tip of the South American mainland. Pigafetta reported that the explorer fell to his knees and sobbed.

Now Magellan had proved his skills, navigating through a fiendish maze of inlets, bays, and deadly currents. The fleet had earlier lost the *Santiago*, sunk but with the crew rescued, while the *San Antonio* had disappeared, believed to have mutinied. But Magellan had discovered a path into a new ocean, which he named *Pacifico*, meaning "peaceful."

A member of Magellan's crew views the tricky route ahead through the Strait of Magellan, which stretches for 370 mi. (600km).

Crossing the Pacific, the ships' food became riddled with worms and sailors sold or fought over rats to eat. Many crew members died from disease.

Magellan thought it would take only a few days to reach Asia. It took almost four months, in desperate conditions. Timbers split in the heat, which also melted the tar that waterproofed the ships. Drinking water spoiled, and the crew ate rats, sawdust, and the leather strips from sails. In March 1521, the crippled vessels landed on the Mariana Islands, halfway between Japan and Papua New Guinea. Magellan had completed the longest-ever nonstop voyage—7,000 mi. (11,200km) across the Pacific—and all without charts.

After getting more supplies, the fleet sailed west to the Philippines, an archipelago of more than 3,000 islands, none of which were on European maps. They received a friendly welcome, but Magellan became involved in a dispute between warring tribes and fought the islanders of Mactan.

Magellan's 49 men were outnumbered 20 to one. Most fled, leaving him and six sailors to keep the enemy at bay. It did not last. As a spear struck his elbow, Magellan went down under a hail of clubs.

Magellan was killed as his men escaped to their ships. Pigafetta wrote in his journal: "And so they slew . . . our true and only guide."

Without its leader, the voyage descended into chaos. The new captains, Duarte Barbosa and Juan Serrano, were slaughtered with 25 other men on the island of Cebu. Sailors were abandoned or were killed in quarrels. The ships sailed aimlessly for months, but when the crew of the *Trinidad* loaded up greedily with a huge cargo of spices, the vessel sprang leaks and had to stay for repairs. The *Victoria*, now captained by Juan Sebastian del Cano, finally limped home in September 1522. Of the 277 sailors who had set out, only 18 ragged, barefoot men returned to Spain, covered in boils and sores.

Eventually there were too few men to sail three ships, so they set the *Concepción* on fire. The vessel was destroyed, along with all of Magellan's logs.

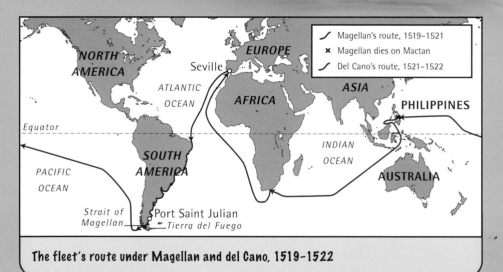

| Magellan's route, 1519–1521 |
| Magellan dies on Mactan |
| Del Cano's route, 1521–1522 |

The fleet's route under Magellan and del Cano, 1519-1522

The value of the *Victoria*'s cargo almost equaled the entire cost of the expedition. More importantly, however, Ferdinand Magellan had organized the first circumnavigation of the planet, proving that Earth is round. He died after completing the toughest part of the voyage, having become the first European to reach Tierra del Fuego, the first to land on the Philippines, and the first to cross the Pacific Ocean.

The exhausted survivors of the *Victoria* reach home. They had sailed more than 42,700 mi. (69,000km)—around ten times the distance of Columbus's first voyage across the Atlantic.

LIFE LINK
Both Ferdinand Magellan and Samuel de Champlain were determined to find a route from the Atlantic Ocean west through the Americas to Asia. While Magellan was convinced that he could reach the Pacific Ocean through South America, de Champlain believed that he could reach China by sailing down the rivers of Canada.

Samuel de Champlain

June 1609. Samuel de Champlain loaded his harquebus, a primitive musketlike gun, with four pieces of shot. He stood on the shore of Lake Champlain, the lake that he had discovered and named. The explorer had been the leader of a war party of ten Frenchmen and around 300 Montagnais, Algonquin, and Huron Native Americans on the hunt for their enemy, the Iroquois.

After several weeks of paddling canoes up the Richelieu River without sighting their foes, most of the armed force had returned home. De Champlain, two other Frenchmen, and around 60 Native Americans were all that remained. Facing them were more than 200 hostile Iroquois warriors, ready for battle.

De Champlain identified the Iroquois chiefs by their headdresses, which loomed larger than those of the other warriors.

The Iroquois were only 100 ft. (30m) away. Samuel de Champlain spotted their three chiefs in a group, and as the Iroquois reached for their bows, he fired. A roar exploded from his harquebus, and two of the enemy fell. Arrows rained down from both sides. Sixteen of de Champlain's group lay wounded. Another harquebus fired. The Iroquois had never seen such a weapon. They began to retreat, fleeing into the forests and pursued by de Champlain's men, who took a dozen Iroquois prisoner. Victory was celebrated with a feast of plundered Iroquois food. It was the first of a series of clashes between French settlers and the Iroquois that would last for almost 100 years.

De Champlain grew up in the town of Brouage, on France's Atlantic coast. He was often taken out to sea by his father, a ship captain, but never learned how to swim because he thought it was too dangerous. He fought in the army as a young man and made his first journey across the Atlantic between 1599 and 1601. The voyage took him to many parts of the Spanish Empire in the Americas, from Colombia to Puerto Rico and, inland, to Mexico City. His account of the voyage was read by King Henry IV of France, who appointed de Champlain to the position of royal hydrographer, or sea geographer.

He arrived in North America for the first time in 1603. He had endured a stormy ten-week voyage onboard a ship chartered by the French to explore lands that might be suitable for fur trading. At that time, a large part of the region now part of Canada and the United States was known as New France.

De Champlain spent two and a half years in Central America and northern South America. He was horrified to see the native peoples treated so badly by European explorers.

De Champlain learned how to navigate ships from his father. He was a skilled mapmaker, too.

De Champlain fought for Prince Henry of Navarre against Spain. In 1589 the prince was crowned King Henry IV of France.

In 1611 de Champlain became only the second European to ride the treacherous Lachine rapids in a canoe. The first had been Etienne Brûlé, who later became de Champlain's scout.

In New France, de Champlain charted the Saint Lawrence River and mapped 930 mi. (1,500km) of Atlantic coastline. He remembered how brutally the Spanish had treated the peoples of Central America—and chose a different path. He formed an alliance with native groups, such as the Montagnais and Huron, against the warlike Iroquois, whose raids threatened both the French and the northern native peoples. The explorer hoped that, with his allies' help, he would be able to set up permanent French settlements. His first settlement was established on Saint Croix Island in 1604, but the harsh winter took its toll, killing 35 of the 79 settlers. The survivors moved to a new location, Port Royal, on the peninsula of Nova Scotia.

The settlers of Saint Croix were decimated by a mystery disease. Much later, de Champlain learned that they had been killed by scurvy, caused by a lack of fresh fruit and vegetables.

In 1608 de Champlain led around 30 colonists to form a settlement on the banks of the Saint Lawrence River. Life was harsh, and only de Champlain and eight others survived the first bitter winter, with many dying of scurvy or smallpox. The settlement, called Québec, struggled for many years but would later develop into one of Canada's largest cities.

De Champlain's expeditions in New France, 1603–1616

NEW FRANCE

Québec
Saint Croix
Port Royal
Lake Champlain
Ottawa
ATLANTIC OCEAN
Lake Huron
Lake Ontario
Cape Cod

1603–1607
1608–1616

In case of attack, de Champlain fortified the first settlement in Québec with a strong wooden barricade.

In late 1615 de Champlain was injured by an Iroquois arrow. He recovered during the winter with the Huron tribes, taking notes about their ways of life.

With the help of local tribes, de Champlain ventured deeper into northern North America than any European had done before him. In bark-covered canoes he explored the Richelieu River, Lake Champlain, and the Ottawa River. He crossed Lake Ontario and reached Lake Huron in August 1615. But his explorations came to an end after he was badly wounded that winter.

De Champlain worked hard to maintain the colonies, sailing to and from France to raise money. After four years in exile while New France was ruled by the English, he returned to Québec in 1633 as the governor of the territory. In all, he made 26 transatlantic crossings, and his bold expeditions laid a path for waves of future settlers and explorers of North America.

LIFE LINK
Samuel de Champlain founded Québec in 1608. 150 years later, the city was besieged by British forces. One of the sailors who had the job of providing accurate charts of the river for the British navy was James Cook.

James Cook

June 11, 1770. The *Endeavour*'s timbers ground against the razor-sharp coral. Water poured in from gashes in the ship's hull, more than the three pumps could cope with. The vessel was in danger of breaking apart, but abandoning ship was not an option—the boats onboard would hold only half the crew . . .

When his ship ran aground, Lieutenant James Cook had been navigating the "insane labyrinth" of coral reefs and islands of the Great Barrier Reef. It took hours of feverish work to wrestle the *Endeavour* free. The holes were plugged with spare sailcloth, and finally the ship limped away.

Six weeks earlier, in a cove he later named Botany Bay, Cook had led ashore a small group of rowboats. With the words "Isaac, you shall land first," Cook summoned forward 16-year-old midshipman Isaac Smith, his nephew, to become the first European to set foot on the eastern shore of Australia.

To free the *Endeavour* from the reef, Cook commanded his men to throw six guns and 50 tons of drinking water overboard in order to lighten the ship.

As a young boy, Cook worked in a grocer's in the English fishing village of Staithes. He loved to listen to sailors' tales around the harbor and at the Cod and Lobster Inn.

Following a career in the merchant navy, Cook had joined the British Royal Navy as an able seaman (ordinary sailor) at the age of 27. He was praised for his accurate mapmaking in Canada, and in 1768 he set off on the greatest voyage of his career—an expedition to the newly discovered island of Tahiti in the southern Pacific Ocean to observe the planet Venus passing in front of the Sun.

The *Endeavour* sailed from the British port of Plymouth on August 26, 1768. Onboard were 85 men, including a one-handed cook, John Thompson, and several scientists, among them Joseph Banks. Banks brought with him four servants, 150 books, and two greyhounds. The dogs joined chickens, pigs, and even a goat that had journeyed around the world with the explorer Samuel Wallis.

The route took the ship through stormy southern Atlantic seas, around Cape Horn at South America's southern tip, and into the mighty Pacific Ocean. The scientists collected plants and animals almost every day by trawling for fish or exploring on land. Banks even shot a giant albatross shortly before Christmas day. Many of the crew were upset, but the bird was roasted and eaten regardless.

At age 18, Cook joined the merchant navy to work on boats carrying coal across the North Sea.

The *Endeavour* reached the coast of Australia 20 months after setting sail from Great Britain. Midshipman Isaac Smith was the first to land, with Cook following close behind.

The *Endeavour* reached Tahiti in April 1769. During the three-month stay, Venus was observed and the coast mapped. The Tahitians were so friendly that two crew members tried to stay behind with native women, while Banks and William Monkhouse, a surgeon, almost fought a pistol duel over another woman.

Cook was unhappy about his men's behavior. Unlike many other explorers who plundered and murdered, he tried to build good relations with the islanders. This was not easy with the warlike Maori tribes at their next landing point—New Zealand. Abel Tasman had discovered the country in 1642, but Cook was the first person to circle its entire coastline and discover that it was made up of two islands. Cook then sailed to Van Diemen's Land (now known as Tasmania) and on to the eastern coast of New Holland (modern-day Australia).

After leaving Tahiti, Cook opened secret orders from the British navy instructing him to search for the fabled continent of *Terra Australis Incognita*—"the unknown land of the south."

Naturalists Daniel Solander and Joseph Banks studied many previously unknown species of wildlife in Australia, including "jumping wild dogs" (kangaroos) and koalas.

Cook's men were among the first Europeans to see tattooed Maori warriors. Some crew members had tattoos done on their arms, starting a tradition among sailors that lasted for centuries.

The expedition charted more than 1,800 mi. (3,000km) of Australia's coast and collected more than 1,000 specimens of new plants and animals. But the near shipwreck on the Great Barrier Reef took its toll. The ship was in a sorry state, with its worn hull only three millimeters thick in places. Cook was forced to dock for repairs in Batavia (modern-day Jakarta, Indonesia). The disease-ridden port swarmed with malaria-carrying mosquitoes. Cook's crew suffered horribly, and by the time they reached Cape Town, South Africa, 33 men had died. The *Endeavour* pressed on but was so ravaged by the seas that parts of the rigging were falling apart. The battered ship eventually reached Great Britain on April 13, 1771.

Cook returned to his modest home in the East End of London to find that two of his children had died while he was at sea. He was promoted to the rank of Master and Commander but earned ship's pay of only £105 ($200) for the entire three-year voyage.

Cook's three voyages, 1768-1779

The men ate sauerkraut (fermented cabbage), limes, and other fruit to stave off scurvy.

Cook was devastated to lose so many men to dysentery and other diseases in Batavia.

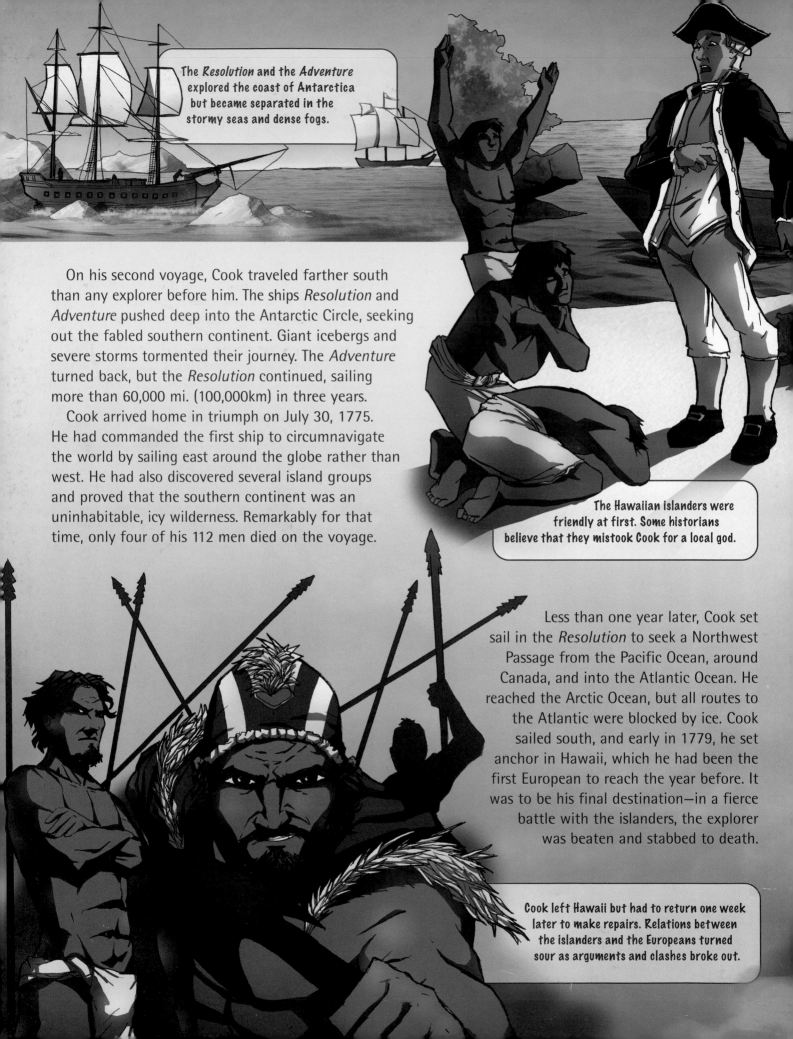

The *Resolution* and the *Adventure* explored the coast of Antarctica but became separated in the stormy seas and dense fogs.

On his second voyage, Cook traveled farther south than any explorer before him. The ships *Resolution* and *Adventure* pushed deep into the Antarctic Circle, seeking out the fabled southern continent. Giant icebergs and severe storms tormented their journey. The *Adventure* turned back, but the *Resolution* continued, sailing more than 60,000 mi. (100,000km) in three years.

Cook arrived home in triumph on July 30, 1775. He had commanded the first ship to circumnavigate the world by sailing east around the globe rather than west. He had also discovered several island groups and proved that the southern continent was an uninhabitable, icy wilderness. Remarkably for that time, only four of his 112 men died on the voyage.

The Hawaiian islanders were friendly at first. Some historians believe that they mistook Cook for a local god.

Less than one year later, Cook set sail in the *Resolution* to seek a Northwest Passage from the Pacific Ocean, around Canada, and into the Atlantic Ocean. He reached the Arctic Ocean, but all routes to the Atlantic were blocked by ice. Cook sailed south, and early in 1779, he set anchor in Hawaii, which he had been the first European to reach the year before. It was to be his final destination—in a fierce battle with the islanders, the explorer was beaten and stabbed to death.

Cook left Hawaii but had to return one week later to make repairs. Relations between the islanders and the Europeans turned sour as arguments and clashes broke out.

On February 14, 1779 Cook's men opened fire on a crowd of angry Hawaiians, who charged at them with raised clubs.

LIFE LINK
One of the scientists on James Cook's second voyage was Georg Forster. His report of the expedition was read by the teenage Alexander von Humboldt, who was so inspired that he met Forster and traveled with him throughout Europe in 1790. Years later, von Humboldt dedicated his greatest work, *Kosmos*, to Forster.

Cook was not the first European to reach Australia, New Zealand, or a number of the Pacific islands he visited. But he was the first to survey them in depth, while the scientists studied the lands, wildlife, and peoples. Nine years after Cook's death, European settlers landed in Botany Bay. Their settlement grew into Australia's largest city, Sydney.

Cook's widow, Elizabeth, outlived her husband by 56 years, sharing a house with her nephew. He became an admiral, but as a teenager, Isaac Smith had been the boy summoned by James Cook to be the first of his crew to set foot in Australia.

Cook tried to flee but was killed in a violent battle at the water's edge. His body was buried at sea.

Alexander von Humboldt

May 1800. Deep in the jungles of South America, the local poison master beckoned Alexander von Humboldt to follow him. The young explorer's eyes and throat burned from the smoke mixed with the smell of roasting flesh. Earlier, under the poison master's instruction, he had taken his first taste of curare—a powerful poison that can kill a bird in three minutes, a pig in ten minutes, and a man in a little longer. Von Humboldt believed that the deadly substance was safe if swallowed; it had to enter the bloodstream directly in order to kill. He had taken quite a gamble to prove his theory.

Von Humboldt and his companion, Aimé Bonpland, were thousands of miles from home, entering the huts of a rainforest tribe near La Esmeralda (now in Venezuela). Through the gloom, von Humboldt saw what was being cooked and turned away, revolted. *They eat their own children*, he thought, only to discover that the bodies roasting on the fire were types of monkeys never before seen by Europeans. Bonpland took a roasted arm back to Europe; it was so well preserved that it lasted for many years.

Von Humboldt and Bonpland enter a rainforest village in the Amazon. They were the first Europeans to see curare harvested from trees and used as a poison. Von Humboldt would take back samples to Europe for other scientists to experiment with.

When his mother died in 1796, von Humboldt inherited a large fortune and was able to finance his own travels. He was denied the chance to travel with Napoleon's army to explore Egypt, however, and he then tried to join Nicolas Baudin's expedition around the world. To von Humboldt's frustration, the voyage was postponed, but by then he had befriended a French botanist, Aimé Bonpland. The pair traveled to Madrid, Spain, seeking permission from the king, Charles II, to explore South America.

As a child, von Humboldt was often sick. After his tutor read *Robinson Crusoe* to him, he began to dream of becoming an explorer.

Von Humboldt was born into a wealthy family in the Prussian town of Tegel (in modern-day Germany). As a young boy, he was fascinated with the natural world, collecting rocks, fossils, and plants, but his mother insisted that he study finance and law. At college in Göttingen, von Humboldt went to as many scientific lectures as he could. He also met Georg Forster, a veteran of James Cook's second voyage, and threw himself into the study of foreign languages and geology.

In 1790 Georg Forster took the young von Humboldt under his wing on a hiking trip across northern Europe. In England they met the famous naturalist Joseph Banks, who had been a key member of Captain Cook's first voyage to the Pacific Ocean.

Still in their 20s, von Humboldt and Bonpland set sail in June 1799 on a journey into the unknown. The coasts of South America were well charted, but most of the interior remained unmapped.

Many sailors died from typhoid fever on the voyage, but the outbreak didn't stop von Humboldt and Bonpland from charting the night sky and taking hundreds of measurements from the seawater they collected.

On the South American mainland, the explorers cataloged their first sample, a mangrove tree, before they had even unloaded their luggage. Wildly excited, Humboldt wrote, "Fantastic plants, electric eels, armadillos, monkeys, parrots . . . We've been running around like a couple of mad things!"

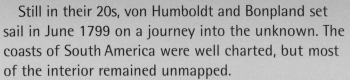

The explorers arrived in Venezuela with 42 scientific instruments, including telescopes, thermometers, microscopes, and a hygrometer.

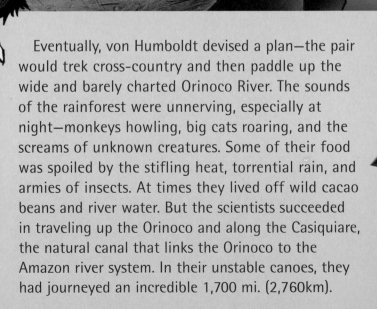

Eventually, von Humboldt devised a plan—the pair would trek cross-country and then paddle up the wide and barely charted Orinoco River. The sounds of the rainforest were unnerving, especially at night—monkeys howling, big cats roaring, and the screams of unknown creatures. Some of their food was spoiled by the stifling heat, torrential rain, and armies of insects. At times they lived off wild cacao beans and river water. But the scientists succeeded in traveling up the Orinoco and along the Casiquiare, the natural canal that links the Orinoco to the Amazon river system. In their unstable canoes, they had journeyed an incredible 1,700 mi. (2,760km).

Von Humboldt collected electric eels from the Orinoco River and placed them in a barrel. He could not resist sticking in his hand, which gave him an electric shock.

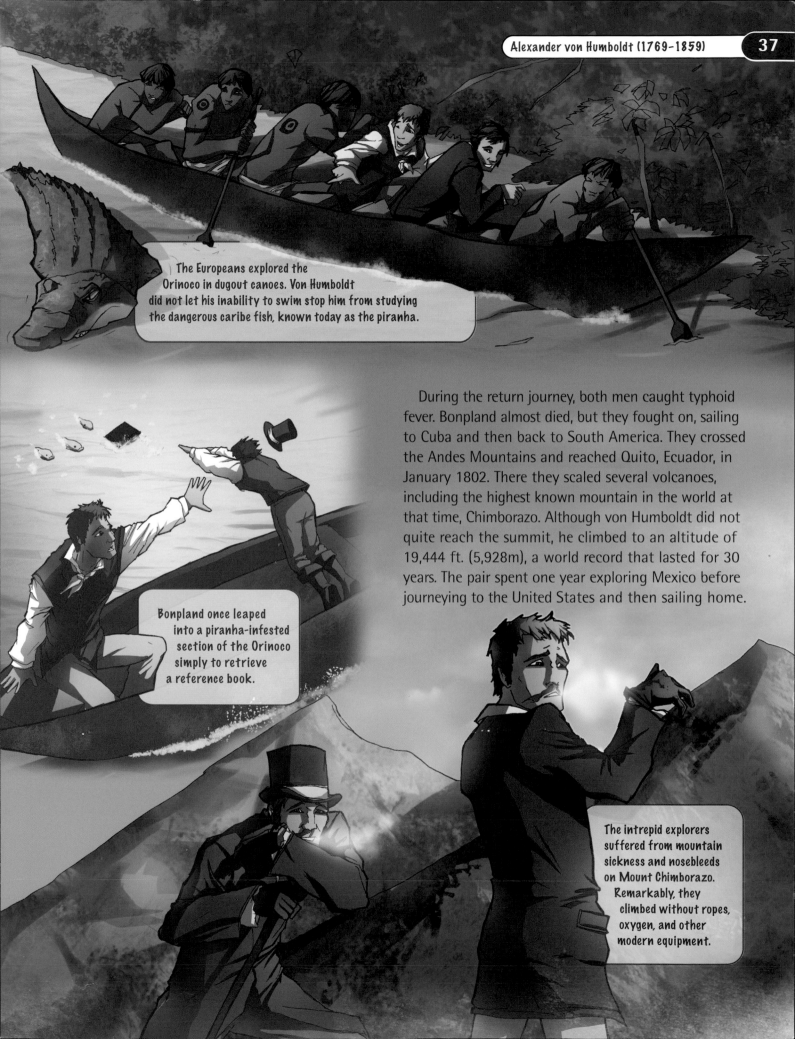

The Europeans explored the Orinoco in dugout canoes. Von Humboldt did not let his inability to swim stop him from studying the dangerous caribe fish, known today as the piranha.

During the return journey, both men caught typhoid fever. Bonpland almost died, but they fought on, sailing to Cuba and then back to South America. They crossed the Andes Mountains and reached Quito, Ecuador, in January 1802. There they scaled several volcanoes, including the highest known mountain in the world at that time, Chimborazo. Although von Humboldt did not quite reach the summit, he climbed to an altitude of 19,444 ft. (5,928m), a world record that lasted for 30 years. The pair spent one year exploring Mexico before journeying to the United States and then sailing home.

Bonpland once leaped into a piranha-infested section of the Orinoco simply to retrieve a reference book.

The intrepid explorers suffered from mountain sickness and nosebleeds on Mount Chimborazo. Remarkably, they climbed without ropes, oxygen, and other modern equipment.

During their five-year expedition, von Humboldt and Bonpland traveled 5,950 mi. (9,600km) on horseback, in canoes, and on foot. They collected or described 6,300 plant and animal species unknown in Europe and proved that the Orinoco and Amazon river systems are joined. They also explored how the warm ocean current off the western coast of South America (now known as the Humboldt Current) influences the weather of Peru, Chile, and Ecuador.

Von Humboldt settled in Paris, France, the capital of the scientific world, where he was showered with honors. The great philosopher Johann Wolfgang von Goethe declared that "One learned more from an hour in his company than eight days of studying books." Von Humboldt lived simply and was modest about his achievements. He helped young scientists and performed many experiments—he was the first person to describe magnetic storms and seismic waves, he invented the term *Jurassic*, and he also investigated the gases that make up our planet's atmosphere.

Von Humboldt's expedition to the Americas, 1799–1804

The scientists catalog samples in the jungle. Despite the hardships of the journey, they wore fashionable European clothes at all times.

In 1827 von Humboldt returned to Prussia, his home country, to work as the king's chief adviser on science. At the age of 60, he set off on a 9,300-mi. (15,000-km)-long trek through Russia, during which he discovered diamonds in the Ural Mountains. Sixteen years later, he began his most ambitious project of all—to condense the scientific knowledge of Earth and the universe into a series of books called *Kosmos*. Von Humboldt believed that all forces and life on Earth are connected and depend on one another, which was a revolutionary idea at that time. While working on the fifth volume, he died in Berlin at the age of 89.

Von Humboldt was one of the first explorers to travel purely out of scientific interest, with no desire for power, glory, or riches. He influenced people as diverse as Charles Darwin and the South American freedom fighter Simón Bolívar. Bolívar declared that "Humboldt was the true discoverer of America because his work has produced more benefit to our people than all the conquistadors." Darwin simply called him "the greatest scientific traveler that ever lived."

French Emperor Napoleon met von Humboldt several times but was so suspicious of the scientist that he had him followed by the secret police and almost expelled from France.

As he wrote, von Humboldt would cover the table in his Paris home with notes. From time to time a carpenter would simply plane the surface clean.

LIFE LINK
After leaving Latin America, Alexander von Humboldt sailed to the U.S. in 1804 to visit President Thomas Jefferson. The two men met several times and discussed the progress of Meriwether Lewis's expedition, which had been organized by Jefferson and set off six days before von Humboldt's arrival in the U.S.

Meriwether Lewis

It all began with the world's biggest-ever land purchase. In 1803 the United States bought the Louisiana Territory from France for $15 million. This vast area measured around one million sq. mi. (two million sq km)—bigger than all of Mexico and four times the size of France. At once, the U.S. doubled in size.

Most of this land was unexplored. The American president, Thomas Jefferson, ordered an expedition that would travel along the Missouri River to its source and then cross the Rocky Mountains to reach the Pacific Ocean. Its leader was to be Jefferson's private secretary, Captain Meriwether Lewis. As his joint commander, Lewis recommended Lieutenant William Clark, the man he had served under in the army.

In 1803 Lewis (left) and Clark took charge of a unit of 12 men called the Corps of Discovery. The Corps grew to around 40 members before it set off from Saint Louis.

For the first five months, the Corps of Discovery traveled up the Missouri River in a keelboat, or barge, and two smaller boats called pirogues.

Moving against the current was a struggle. Sometimes crew members used long poles to push the keelboat upriver, while teams on the bank pulled the pirogues by rope.

The explorers almost died of starvation during an 11-day trek across the hostile Bitterroot Range.

Lewis and Clark set out from Saint Louis, on the eastern edge of the Louisiana Territory, in the spring of 1804. They traveled up the Missouri, battling the river's flow in a barge, two pirogues, and, later on, small canoes. Often the boats had to be towed ashore and carried because the river was too fierce to navigate. Other hazards included the tough terrain, wolves and grizzly bears, swarms of mosquitoes, and some hostile Native Americans. But in general, the explorers developed friendly relationships with the tribes, giving gifts and making welcoming speeches.

The terrain grew tougher as the expedition pressed on into the vast Rocky Mountains. Without friendly Native Americans who traded supplies and knowledge, it would have been doomed. The Nez Perce people, for example, greeted the exhausted and starving explorers after they had almost died crossing the snow-covered Bitterroot Range. The tribesmen could have slaughtered the helpless group and taken their weapons and supplies. Instead, they fed and cared for the party.

Leaving their horses with the Nez Perce, Lewis and Clark used dugout canoes to travel downstream along the Clearwater, Snake, and Columbia rivers. The journey was hazardous, cold, and wet. Finally, in November 1805, they reached the western coast of the U.S. and set their eyes on the Pacific Ocean.

After reaching the coast, Clark wrote in his journal: "Great joy in camp; we are in view of this great Pacific Ocean, which we have been so long anxious to see."

Lewis and Clark spent the winter in Fort Clatsop, preparing for the return home. On the outward trip, many tribes had refused to accept paper money or a note of trade signed by President Jefferson, so the explorers relied on bartering goods, including 36 tomahawk axes. Now they were short of items to trade. In desperation, they stole a canoe and bartered away their brass coat buttons. Clark even posed as a doctor, selling his services for supplies.

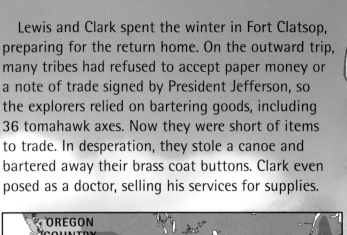

The Corps of Discovery built Fort Clatsop close to the Pacific. There, they recovered from illnesses, hunted elk for food, and made leather clothing for the journey home.

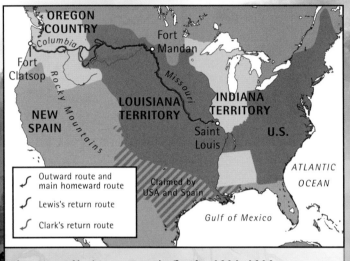

Lewis and Clark's route to the Pacific, 1804-1806

OREGON COUNTRY
Columbia
Fort Clatsop
Fort Mandan
Rocky Mountains
Missouri
NEW SPAIN
LOUISIANA TERRITORY
INDIANA TERRITORY
Saint Louis
U.S.
ATLANTIC OCEAN
Claimed by USA and Spain
Gulf of Mexico

〜 Outward route and main homeward route
〜 Lewis's return route
〜 Clark's return route

The expedition split into two groups in order to chart as much land as possible. Lewis's team included Pierre Cruzatte, a fur trader whose cheery fiddle playing had helped keep morale high. But the trader was very nearsighted and almost killed Lewis while the pair hunted elk, shooting his leader in the rear end by accident. Lewis endured a painful journey back to Saint Louis but did not punish Cruzatte for his error.

Lewis and Clark relied on the local knowledge and interpreting skills of Sacagawea, the Native American wife of a French fur trader.

With his rifle unloaded, Lewis once survived the threat of a grizzly bear attack by fleeing into a river.

The two groups reunited in August 1806 at the Missouri River and received a heroes' welcome on their return to Saint Louis one month later. They had been gone so long that they were feared dead. Remarkably, only one member of the group had died—Sergeant Charles Floyd, of a burst appendix.

Although Lewis and Clark had not found an easy path to the Pacific Ocean, the legacy of their trek was enormous. They helped the American people increase their knowledge of their huge new country, describing several hundred plant and animal species. They reported on or met with around 50 different Native American tribes—including the Sioux, Lakota, Blackfoot, and Chinook—and forged friendly relationships with most of them. And Clark's accurate maps would prove invaluable to the legions of American pioneers who headed west in the following 100 years.

Lewis, wearing his army uniform, leads the Corps of Discovery in greeting a Blackfoot chief. After the epic journey, he was appointed the governor of the Lousiana Territory, but he died only three years later.

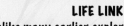

LIFE LINK
Unlike many earlier explorers, Meriwether Lewis built friendly relationships with native peoples. To do this, he relied on interpreters like Sacagawea. The success of Richard Burton's expeditions also depended on his mastery of native languages in order to gain vital information from local peoples.

Richard Burton

Scoundrel and scholar, ruffian and hero—the life of Richard Francis Burton reads like the most thrilling adventure story. As a child, he lived in France, Great Britain, and Italy and picked up foreign languages with amazing ease. He was a fiercely intelligent but unruly student at Oxford University, where he quickly made his mark. In his first term, Burton challenged a fellow student—who had made fun of his huge mustache—to a sword duel. He avoided the subjects that he was supposed to study, instead learning Arabic and taking up fencing and falconry.

When the hotheaded Burton was expelled from Oxford University in 1842, he was said to have ridden his carriage over the flower beds of Trinity College as he left.

After seven years working for the British army as a soldier, interpreter, and undercover agent in India, Burton embarked on his most daring expedition. His destination was Mecca (Saudi Arabia), the holiest city in the Muslim world. He set off in April 1853, disguised as a Muslim doctor. Burton knew that a mistake would be deadly—Mecca was a place where non-Muslims, if caught, could expect to be beheaded.

As a soldier in India, Burton's fierce style of fighting earned him the nickname Ruffian Dick.

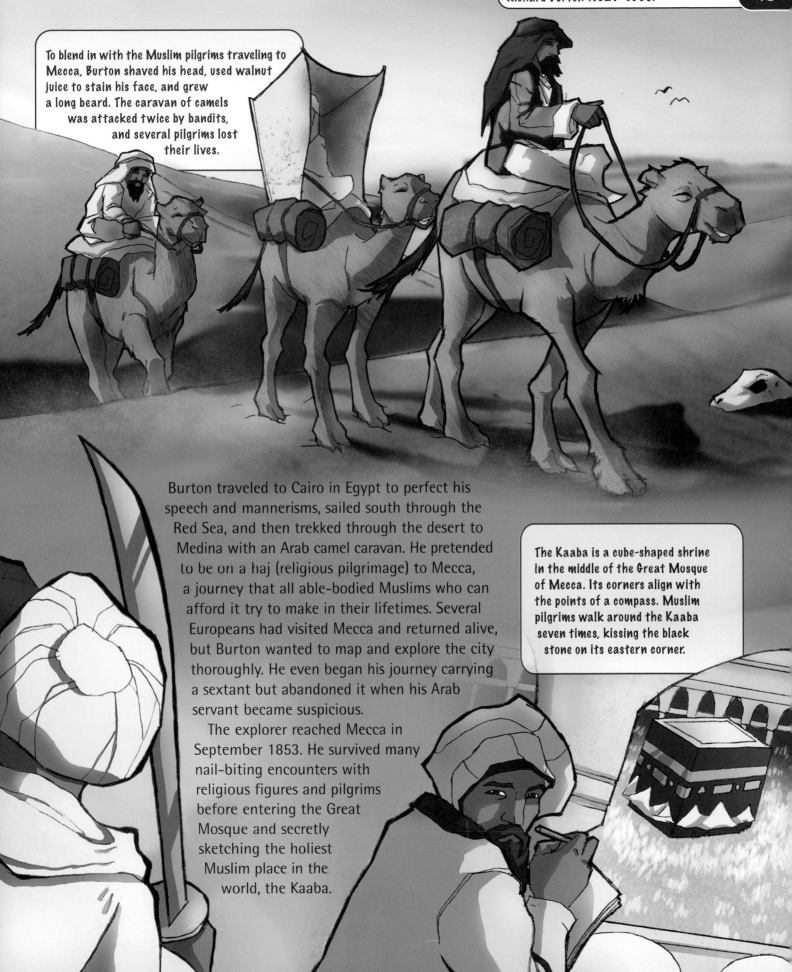

To blend in with the Muslim pilgrims traveling to Mecca, Burton shaved his head, used walnut juice to stain his face, and grew a long beard. The caravan of camels was attacked twice by bandits, and several pilgrims lost their lives.

Burton traveled to Cairo in Egypt to perfect his speech and mannerisms, sailed south through the Red Sea, and then trekked through the desert to Medina with an Arab camel caravan. He pretended to be on a haj (religious pilgrimage) to Mecca, a journey that all able-bodied Muslims who can afford it try to make in their lifetimes. Several Europeans had visited Mecca and returned alive, but Burton wanted to map and explore the city thoroughly. He even began his journey carrying a sextant but abandoned it when his Arab servant became suspicious.

The explorer reached Mecca in September 1853. He survived many nail-biting encounters with religious figures and pilgrims before entering the Great Mosque and secretly sketching the holiest Muslim place in the world, the Kaaba.

The Kaaba is a cube-shaped shrine in the middle of the Great Mosque of Mecca. Its corners align with the points of a compass. Muslim pilgrims walk around the Kaaba seven times, kissing the black stone on its eastern corner.

One year later, in 1854, Burton set out for another sacred Muslim site, the city of Harar (now in Ethiopia) in east Africa. Again he risked execution if discovered as a nonbeliever, but the danger seemed to inspire him. After several narrow escapes, the fearless explorer became the first white man to both visit the city and come out alive.

After leaving Harar, Burton almost died of thirst but managed to follow the flight of desert birds to find water.

Hostile Somali tribesmen attacked Burton's camp in Berbera in April 1855. The surprise assault took place in the middle of the night.

Burton's next serious brush with death came during another African expedition. Deep in Somalia with his companions John Hanning Speke and William Stroyan, the explorers were attacked by around 200 local tribespeople. Stroyan was killed and his body mutilated, while Speke survived 11 spear and club wounds. Fighting with a saber, Burton was struck in the face by a javelin spear. The weapon stayed in place as Burton battled and eventually escaped with Speke. Barely able to speak or eat, he struggled back to Great Britain to endure a long and painful recovery.

The spear stabbed through Burton's cheek, smashed four teeth and part of his jaw, and then pierced his other cheek.

As restless as ever, Burton turned his attention to the heart of Africa, known at the time as the Dark Continent. He planned to find the source of the mighty Nile, the longest river in the world.

Burton set off with Speke from the island of Zanzibar, landed in Bagamoyo, Tanzania, on the east African coast in June 1857, and ventured inland. The terrain was rugged and the climate hot and humid, making the five-month, 600-mi. (1,000-km)-long trek to Kazeh exhausting. Both men caught malaria but refused to give up as they pushed westward, crossing the hills of Unyamwezi.

In February 1858, Burton and Speke stumbled down to the shore of Lake Tanganyika. They had found Africa's second-largest lake but were disappointed to find that the Rusizi, the river at its northern tip, was not a source of the Nile. On the journey back, they heard about another great lake to the north.

Burton was still ill, but Speke set off and found Lake Victoria, Africa's largest lake and one of the sources of the Nile River.

During the tortuous 225-day trek across east Africa, Burton lost the use of his legs and had to be carried by native men. Speke went blind and also deaf from a beetle that had burrowed inside his ear.

Sick and exhausted, Burton managed to explore parts of Lake Tanganyika in a dugout canoe.

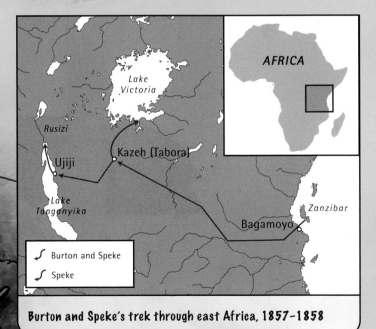

AFRICA

Lake Victoria

Rusizi

Kazeh (Tabora)

Ujiji

Lake Tanganyika

Zanzibar

Bagamoyo

🎐 Burton and Speke
🎐 Speke

Burton and Speke's trek through east Africa, 1857–1858

As Burton stood on the stage, ready for the debate with Speke, he received news of his rival's death on a hunting trip.

In January 1861, Burton married Isabel Arundell in a London church. She traveled around the world with him for almost 30 years.

Burton and Speke traveled separately back to Great Britain. When Burton reached London in May 1859, he found that Speke had taken most of the credit for the success of their expedition. The bad blood between the pair continued for the next five years.

A debate between the two men was planned in 1864 but never took place—Speke had been killed by a gunshot wound. Although Speke appeared to have fired the gun himself, whether it was an accident or a suicide remains a mystery.

During the 1860s, Burton worked as a diplomat in South America. He explored parts of Brazil, Paraguay, Peru, and Argentina.

Although Burton is most famous for his pilgrimages to Muslim holy cities and his explorations of east Africa, he ventured to many other parts of the world. His insatiable curiosity about unfamiliar peoples and places led him to visit the Mormons of Salt Lake City, Utah, and travel through Argentina, Peru, and Paraguay. He also worked as an unlikely diplomat in west Africa, Brazil, Syria, and Trieste (now in Italy), where he died in 1890.

Despite the scandal and controversy that surrounded Burton, he was knighted by Queen Victoria in 1886.

Burton was a great writer, but sadly many of his unpublished journals and diaries were destroyed by his wife after his death.

Amazingly, Burton also found time to write a vast number of books on many different subjects, including ones that shocked Victorian society. He took great delight in telling terrible and often untrue tales about himself but was deeply serious when writing about the countries that he had explored. He translated several texts from the Arabic and Sanskrit languages into English and contributed a great deal to the European knowledge and understanding of the geography and peoples of Africa, the Middle East, and Asia.

LIFE LINK
Richard Burton's greatest expeditions were sponsored by the Royal Geographical Society. One of its founders was John Franklin, who disappeared in 1844 while searching for the Northwest Passage. His exploits inspired Roald Amundsen to become an explorer. Unlike Franklin, however, Amundsen did find a route through the passage.

Roald Amundsen

September 9, 1910. The 19-man crew of the *Fram* relaxed while their ship lay docked at the Atlantic island of Madeira, Portugal. The weather was warm, in contrast to the ship's destination—deep into the icy Arctic Circle to conduct a scientific survey. The top crew, mostly Norwegian and including many veterans of polar voyages, were suddenly called on deck.

As a young medical student, Amundsen neglected his work in order to prepare for life as a polar explorer. He toughened up by cross-country skiing for many hours without sleeping.

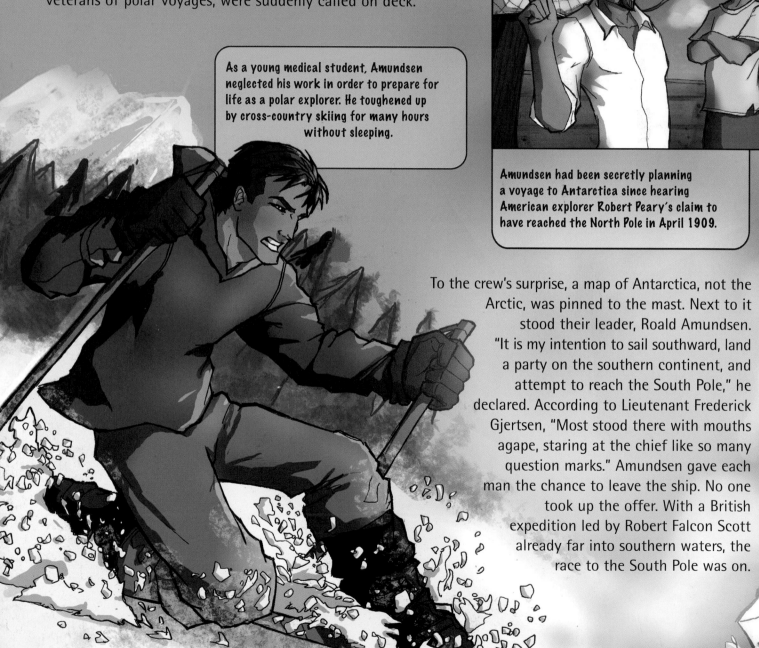

Amundsen had been secretly planning a voyage to Antarctica since hearing American explorer Robert Peary's claim to have reached the North Pole in April 1909.

To the crew's surprise, a map of Antarctica, not the Arctic, was pinned to the mast. Next to it stood their leader, Roald Amundsen. "It is my intention to sail southward, land a party on the southern continent, and attempt to reach the South Pole," he declared. According to Lieutenant Frederick Gjertsen, "Most stood there with mouths agape, staring at the chief like so many question marks." Amundsen gave each man the chance to leave the ship. No one took up the offer. With a British expedition led by Robert Falcon Scott already far into southern waters, the race to the South Pole was on.

By 1910, Amundsen was already an experienced explorer. He had given up his studies to serve aboard polar whaling ships, and at the age of 25 he set off on his first Antarctic expedition (1897–1899) onboard the *Belgica*, which became the first ship to spend a winter in the continent. Four years later, Amundsen was at the other end of the world, commanding a converted fishing trawler, the *Gjøa*, deep into Arctic waters. During the three-year voyage, Amundsen did what his hero, John Franklin, had not managed to do—he found a way through the deadly maze of Arctic Ocean icebergs to sail a Northwest Passage from the Atlantic into the Pacific Ocean.

Amundsen's route through the Northwest Passage, 1903-1906

The *Gjøa* navigates through the Arctic ice. Having found a route through the Northwest Passage, Amundsen left his ship at Herschel Island and skied around 500 mi. (800km) to Eagle City to send a telegram with news of the expedition's success.

Amundsen's next expedition used a custom-built ship, the *Fram*. After leaving Madeira, the sturdy vessel reached the Antarctic coast in January 1911. The crew set up base in the Bay of Whales and built their winter quarters, Framheim. Amundsen equipped his men, all skilled skiers, with warm fur coats like those worn by the Inuit people of the Arctic. They ate well and rested during the long winter and carefully looked after the husky dogs that were supposed to pull their sleds. Olav Bjaaland, a champion skier, was also a carpenter. He decreased the weight of the sleds from 195 lbs. (88kg) to 50 lbs. (22kg). Amundsen's rivals, Scott and his men, used a similar type of sled but did not modify them.

The *Fram* was one of the toughest wooden vessels ever built. Amundsen's team spent three weeks moving ten tons of supplies from the ship to the Framheim camp, 3 mi. (5km) inland.

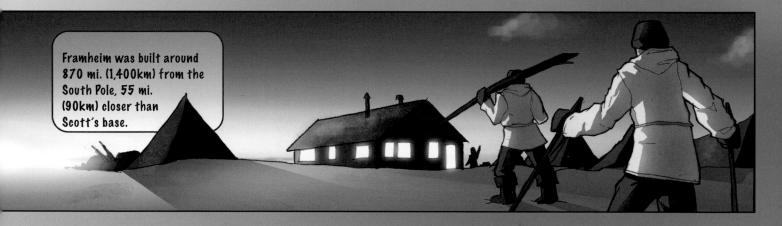

Framheim was built around 870 mi. (1,400km) from the South Pole, 55 mi. (90km) closer than Scott's base.

On October 20, 1911, five men—Amundsen, Bjaaland, Helmer Hanssen, Sverre Hassel, and Oscar Wisting—four sleds, and 52 dogs set out from their base. They averaged 25 mi. (40km) per day for the first few weeks. The sleds were fairly light, since most of the men's food would come from storehouses located along the early part of their route the previous fall.

But progress slowed as they scaled the Queen Maud Mountains and crossed the Devil's Ballroom, a glacier with a thin crust of snow hiding deadly crevasses. Finally they reached the plateau on which the pole lay, but their joy was overshadowed by a terrible task. Some of the huskies were exhausted. More than one half had to be killed and fed to the rest of the pack.

Amundsen's huskies had to be in peak condition in order to reach the pole. A special deck was built on the *Fram* to protect them from the equatorial sun as the ship sailed south. The dogs ate well, while the men's food was rationed.

Amundsen named the fearsome Queen Maud mountain range after the queen of Norway. The huskies struggled to haul the expedition up the steep slopes, two sleds at a time.

On December 14, 1911, Amundsen planted the Norwegian flag on the South Pole. The men built a stone marker and left a letter addressed to the king of Norway, alongside notes of support for Scott. The expedition camera proved to be faulty, but luckily Bjaaland had his own camera to capture pictures of the scene.

After three days on the pole, the team trekked back to base, arriving at Framheim after 99 days and more than 1,800 mi. (2,900km) traveled. All five men survived without major injuries or serious frostbite, but only 11 dogs reached home.

After erecting their flag on the pole, the five men celebrated with cigars and a meal of seal meat. Their usual daily diet was cookies, chocolate, milk powder, and pemmican—a high-calorie mixture of dried meat, berries, and fat.

Scott's five-man team trekked to the pole without dogs. On the return trip, temperatures dropped to −40°F (−40°C). The men suffered from intense frostbite.

In contrast, Scott's trek to the pole was disastrous. Early on, the team's tractors stopped working and their horses had to be shot. Slowed by blizzards, the five men pulled their sleds, reaching the pole 35 days after Amundsen. One can only imagine their despair at arriving second. Low on food, they struggled back in even more hostile conditions. Their frozen bodies were found eight months later, less than 12 mi. (20km) from a supply depot.

Amundsen returned to Norway to great acclaim, but for him the South Pole was only a consolation prize. His main interest was the Arctic, and in 1918 he set out to survey the region. The expedition made some scientific advances, but Amundsen failed in his ambitious plan to lodge his ship in ice and then drift to the North Pole.

During his ill-fated Arctic expedition, Amundsen broke his arm, was poisoned by a faulty gas heater, and was almost mauled to death by a polar bear.

ANTARCTICA
Queen Maud Mountains
South Pole
Lesser Antarctica
Transantarctic Mountains
Amundsen Sea
Ross Ice Shelf
Framheim
Scott's base

ANTARCTICA

⟋ Amundsen's route
⟋ Scott's route
✕ Scott dies on return trip

The race to the South Pole, 1911–1912

Amundsen also explored by air. With Umberto Nobile he flew the *Norge* airship over the North Pole in May 1926. During the 72-hour journey from Norway to Alaska, they traveled 3,383 mi. (5,456km). But the two men argued about who should take credit for the feat. It was the first undisputed sighting of the North Pole (debate still rages over Robert Peary's 1909 claim) and the first flight over the polar icecap from Europe to North America.

On June 18, 1928, Amundsen took off in a seaplane from Tromso, Norway. His mission was to find the stricken crew of Nobile's latest airship, the *Italia*, which had crashed. Some of the survivors were rescued, but the plane carrying Amundsen disappeared. It was never found.

Amundsen's single-mindedness and his quarrels with other explorers lost him many admirers. The British were upset by the way he had treated the huskies in Antarctica. They preferred the heroic but reckless Scott to the cold-hearted Amundsen, who once said, "Adventure is just bad planning." But the Norwegian was a brilliant, intrepid explorer who is celebrated today for his charting of the Northwest Passage and the casualty-free assault on the South Pole.

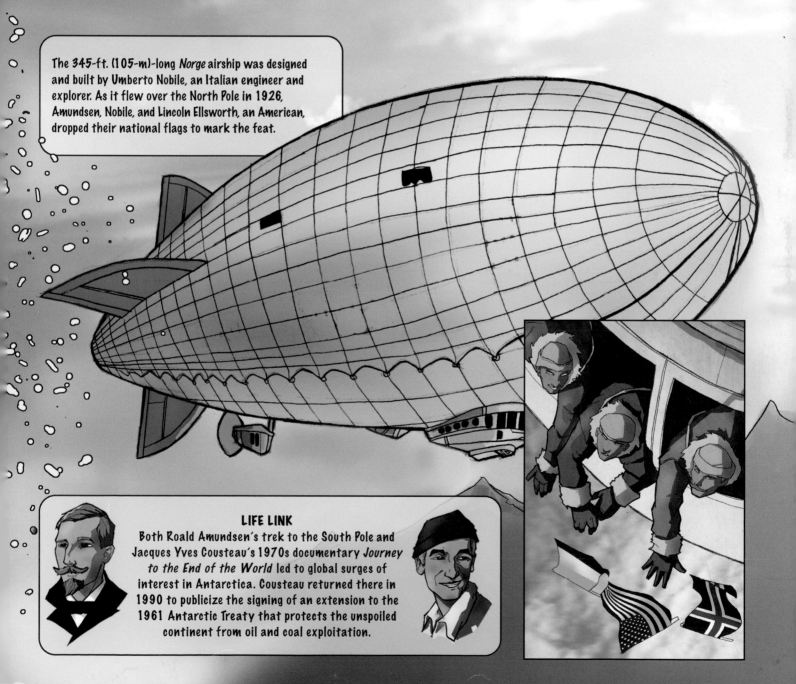

The 345-ft. (105-m)-long *Norge* airship was designed and built by Umberto Nobile, an Italian engineer and explorer. As it flew over the North Pole in 1926, Amundsen, Nobile, and Lincoln Ellsworth, an American, dropped their national flags to mark the feat.

LIFE LINK
Both Roald Amundsen's trek to the South Pole and Jacques Yves Cousteau's 1970s documentary *Journey to the End of the World* led to global surges of interest in Antarctica. Cousteau returned there in 1990 to publicize the signing of an extension to the 1961 Antarctic Treaty that protects the unspoiled continent from oil and coal exploitation.

Jacques Yves Cousteau

Spring 1936. Jacques Yves Cousteau lay on a remote road high up in the Vosges Mountains of eastern France and prepared to die. It was 2 A.M. and his body was shattered. Three broken ribs had punctured his lungs, his left arm was fractured in five places, and his right arm was paralyzed. Blood poured from his wounds.

The French naval cadet had been driving his father's sports car around treacherous hairpin turns when the headlights failed and he crashed. Against the odds, Cousteau was rescued but was in critical condition. It took eight months for him to move just one finger on his paralyzed arm.

As a teenager, Cousteau spent hours dismantling his Pathé movie camera and putting it back together again.

Cousteau's near-fatal accident ended his dream of becoming a naval pilot.

Cousteau spied for the French resistance in World War II, once sneaking into an Italian navy base to photograph top-secret codebooks. He won France's highest military honor for his work.

After leaving the hospital, Cousteau was sent to a naval base in Toulon. There he met Philippe Tailliez, who encouraged him to swim in order to regain strength in his twisted right arm. Tailliez lent Cousteau a pair of swim goggles. Seeing clearly underwater for the first time was a revelation. "Sometimes we are lucky enough to know that our lives have been changed," Cousteau wrote later. "It happened to me that day when my eyes opened to the world beneath the surface of the sea."

Cousteau had always been inquisitive. He was expelled from school for breaking 17 windows in order to test whether a fast- or slow-moving stone left a smaller hole, and by the age of 13 he had shot his first film on an early movie camera. From the late 1930s, Cousteau combined his love of movies with his newfound fascination with the ocean. He teamed up with Tailliez and an artist and spear fisherman named Frédéric "Didi" Dumas. They became known as the Three Musketeers of the Sea. Their innovations and inventions included unmanned mini submarines, live underwater television, and underwater cameras and lights that captured high-quality footage of deep-sea life for the first time.

Cousteau launched his Diving Saucer in 1953. It was a small two-person submarine designed for exploring the seabed.

Cousteau made his most famous invention with Emile Gagnan, an engineer. In 1943 they built an air tank, designed to be worn on a diver's back, that fed compressed air through a special valve. The pressure of the air in the tank matched the pressure of the seawater, meaning that the diver's lungs would not be damaged. The Aqua-Lung, as it was later known, was the first practical, self-contained underwater breathing apparatus (or scuba). Before then, the only way to explore underwater had been in large, expensive diving bells or helmeted diving suits supplied with air from a ship.

Cousteau almost died while testing an early version of the Aqua-Lung that filtered carbon dioxide out of stale air. Fifty feet (15m) down, he managed to rip the device off his back just before he blacked out.

Cousteau's ship *Calypso* was a former minesweeper. It was redesigned as a research vessel by millionaire Loel Guinness. He leased it to Cousteau for one franc per year (less than one dollar).

In the 1950s, Cousteau and his family started making major voyages and feature films. He shot more than 12 mi. (30km) of film in the Mediterranean Sea, the Red Sea, and the Indian Ocean during 1956. The footage was edited down to create *The Silent World*, the first-ever full-length color underwater film.

The movie won an Academy Award and helped Cousteau fund more voyages and television series, including *The Undersea World of Jacques Cousteau*. In 1968 this series brought the mysterious underwater world of rivers, seas, and oceans into millions of homes for the first time.

In 1948 Cousteau and Dumas were trapped deep underwater by three circling sharks. Cousteau used his underwater camera to fend them off until their dive ship came to the rescue. They had only a few breaths of oxygen left.

During 50 years of exploration, the Commander, as Cousteau was nicknamed, made more than 140 movies and documentaries. He traveled more than one million mi. (1.6 million km) around the world and filmed an enormous range of subjects. These included a 2,300-year-old Roman galley (at the time the oldest shipwreck ever discovered) and the remains of the massive ocean liner *Britannic*, the sister ship of the *Titanic*.

Cousteau explored places that had never been seen before by the general public. For example, he made dangerous dives in freezing Antarctic waters to film the dramatic ice structures beneath the waves. Most of his films focused on Earth's rich marine life—battling octopuses and giant squids, highly intelligent dolphins and whales, and even "sleeping" sharks.

As the years passed, Cousteau's movies highlighted the damaging effects of humans on the world's oceans. He campaigned to stop France from dumping radioactive waste in the sea in the 1960s and helped get the 1991 Antarctic Treaty signed to protect the continent from oil drilling and coal mining.

Six years later, Cousteau died. He had won many honors, but most importantly he had inspired millions of people to take an interest in and explore the great rivers, seas, and oceans of our planet.

Cousteau was in charge of Conshelf II, a star-shaped laboratory anchored to the floor of the Red Sea. In 1963 five people lived in the structure for one month.

Cousteau won three Oscars for his amazing documentary movies.

Cousteau appeared in many of his TV documentaries wearing his trademark red woolen hat.

Other famous explorers

Zheng He (1371–c.1433)

Muslim explorer Zheng He was an admiral in the Chinese navy during the Ming dynasty. He sailed on seven major voyages. His first, in 1405, featured 62 ships, some of them more than 500 ft. (140m) long—the largest vessels that the world had seen at that time. He explored Southeast Asia, Sri Lanka, India, Egypt, and Persia (modern-day Iran) and established trade links with more than 25 nations. After his death during a voyage home from India, China scaled down its explorations and became an isolated country once again.

Vasco da Gama (c.1460–1524)

Portugal's Vasco da Gama was the first person to sail from Europe to India around the Cape of Good Hope, the southernmost tip of Africa. His fleet of four ships left Lisbon in July 1497 and encountered turbulent seas and hostile coastal dwellers, while his crew was decimated by scurvy. Da Gama rounded the cape in November and reached India in May 1498. He died of malaria on his third voyage, having helped Portugal set up a power base in the Indian Ocean that would last for almost 500 years.

Francisco Pizarro (c.1475–1541)

From poor beginnings, Francisco Pizarro became the most famous of the Spanish conquistadors who conquered most of Central and South America. He worked as a lowly official in Panama for more than 20 years before heading south on a number of expeditions to search for a fabled empire of great wealth. Pizarro discovered the Inca civilization, brutally defeated them, and then stole most of their gold and destroyed their major cities, including the capital, Cuzco. He set up a new capital in Lima, where he was assassinated following a struggle for power among the conquistadors.

David Livingstone (1813–1873)

Livingstone arrived in Africa to work as a missionary. In 1842 he crossed the Kalahari Desert and was mauled by a lion two years later. For 30 years, Livingstone explored Africa, seeking the source of the Nile River and traveling along most of the Zambezi River. In 1855 he named the Victoria Falls—a huge waterfall more than 330 ft. (100m) high and 1 mi. (1.6km) wide. Rumors of his death prompted the reporter Henry Stanley to search for and find Livingstone in 1872, one year before his death.

Mary Kingsley (1862–1900)

Kingsley left Great Britain in 1893 to travel to parts of Africa that few or no Europeans had ever visited. She explored areas of Angola, Nigeria, and Equatorial Guinea and later trekked through the jungles of the French Congo and Gabon. There she studied the Fang people, who were known to be cannibals. She was one of the first non-Africans to climb Mount Cameroon, an active volcano, but later died of typhoid fever while working as a nurse during the second Boer War.

Glossary

Archipelago A group of islands.

Botanist A scientist who studies plant life.

Cadet A person training to become a member of the armed forces or the police.

Caravan A group of travelers or traders making a journey together over land.

Circumnavigation Traveling all the way around Earth.

City-state A small, independent territory or kingdom based around a large town or city.

Colony A settlement or territory set up by a group of people from a distant country, which is ruled by that country.

Conquistador A Spanish conqueror of the civilizations of Central and South America during the 1400s and 1500s.

Crow's-nest A lookout platform high up on a ship's mast.

Dugout canoe A canoe made by hollowing out a log.

Equator The imaginary line around Earth, halfway between the North and South poles.

Galley A long ship powered by both oars and sails.

Hygrometer An instrument that measures humidity—the amount of water vapor in air.

Log The written record of the trips made by a ship or an aircraft.

Magnetic storm A sudden and severe disturbance of the magnetic field that surrounds Earth.

Malaria An infectious disease spread by the bite of

a certain type of mosquito, causing chills and fever.

Marooned Abandoned in an inhospitable place with little chance of being rescued.

Missionary A person who travels to another country to convert the local peoples to a new religion.

Mutiny A rebellion of sailors against their commanding officers.

Naturalist A scientist who studies animals, plants, or other aspects of the natural world.

Navigate To travel by ship or boat or to plan the course of a journey.

Northwest Passage The sea route from the Atlantic Ocean to the Pacific Ocean through the Arctic waters of northern Canada.

Scurvy A disease caused by lack of vitamin C that makes the sufferer bleed beneath the skin.

Seismic wave A vibration in the ground caused by an earthquake.

Settler A person who travels to live in a new country or a colony.

Sextant An instrument that measures the height of the Sun, used mostly by sailors to figure out their distance from the equator.

Slave trade The business of capturing, trading, and selling people as slaves.

Smallpox An infectious disease that causes a fever and rash.

Strait A narrow sea channel linking two larger areas of water.

Survey To make a map or plan of an area.

Typhoid fever An infectious disease that affects the intestines.

Index